One Unbroken Strand

A collection of love poems

Written by

Janine Holly Earl

authorHOUSE®

AuthorHouse™
1663 Liberty Drive
Bloomington, IN 47403
www.authorhouse.com
Phone: 1 (800) 839-8640

Published by AuthorHouse 11/09/2016

ISBN: 978-1-5246-4738-4 (sc)
ISBN: 978-1-5246-4737-7 (e)

Library of Congress Control Number: 2016917840

Print information available on the last page.

Table of Contents

Acknowledgments to my dear friend Elizabeth Gorek who generously provided her painting for this book cover. 45" x 50" oil on panel titled One Unbroken Strand elizabethgorek.com

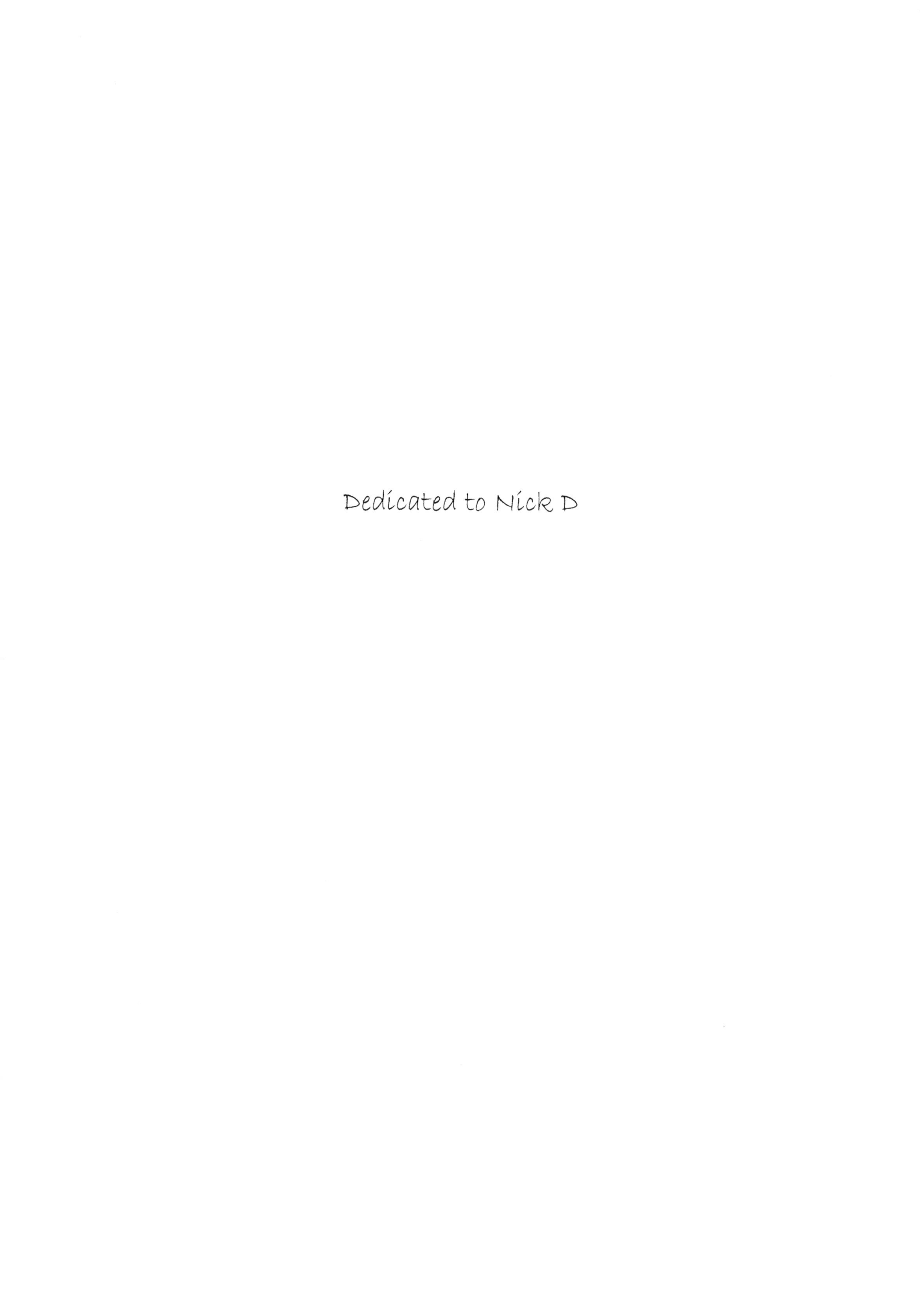

Dedicated to Nick D

A Dark Cloud

I opened like a flower for you
My petals all were wet with dew
We made sweet noises in the night
A passion of the tenderest delight

I was yearning to say I'd be true
You were longing to say adieu
A dark cloud fell upon your face
The light in your eye disappeared without a trace

Now my love is cold and tired
My dear your heart is dried and hard
You will not be my knight and true
Ne'er again will I make love with you
A curse has fallen on this land
Your touch is ice upon my hand

Blossom Tree

There are more answers to your questions
There are more reasons to the changing of the seasons
There is more life here than those who
walk among you can imagine

I've spanned life and death to be by your side
Watched your life like a helpless child
Now my Jane she knows me
Now my Jane believes in who we are again

There is more magic up my sleeve
There is more laughter than you did believe
You've learned your lessons
Felt enough pain
It's time to wander down the lane with no name

I'm a touch a breath a spark away
It's not so far from earth to heaven
I live in the memory of who we were
And who we will be again

There are more answers
To your questions
There are more reasons to the changing of the seasons
There is more life here
Than those who walk among you can imagine

Queen of the Gypsies

There you go with that look in your eye
And I know adventure will be found in the sky
Here I am with all this love in my heart
And all the trouble that you manage to start

And the circle goes around and round
And the circle goes around
Like fairies dancing in the mist
In the mist we twirl around

There you stand with that gun in your back
And it seems to me girl we have wandered too long
When the veil flies over your face
With magic we'll leave no trace

And your skirts of orange and gold twirl round
And your skirts of orange and gold
In the enemy camps we've found
In the enemy camps we've found
And I shall be your clown
And you shall be my queen

Queen of the gypsies
Queen of the rag and bone
The fire we start tonight
Forever be our home

My gypsy woman you are lovely in the night
Your dancing gets us in and out of fights
I've played my fiddle till my fingers bled

My gypsy woman we shall wed
A fort-night from now in your gown of orange and gold
You'll be my bride
Your crystal ball foretold
Our child will have eyes and hair as black as coal

And your skirts of orange and gold twirl
round and your skirts of orange and gold
In the enemy camps we've found we've found
In the enemy camps we've found
And I shall be your clown
And you shall be my Queen

Gossamer Dreams

It's like you've gone to sea for a very long time
I'm at the widow's watch till the end of my life
Seeing is believing, feeling is flight
Heaven at my doorstep, angels in the night

I'll race you to the moon
I'll chase you to the stars
Fill my heart with joy
I'm not doubting anymore

I've been waiting at this party for such a long time
My arms and heart are open and reaching for the sky
Seeing is believing, feeling is flight
Heaven at my doorstep, angels in the night

Sweetness soft like velvet, your skin so smooth
Hair like an angel's all around me,
so deep sinking in my bed
My hands are bound by passion, over under, over me again
Only my soul knows where you take me gossamer dream
I will find you, like the sea find it's shore

Little Tattered Remnant

And all the men are heard to say
Stop your crying and dismay
You weave a web too thick and dark
Your moaning is the pitch of lark

We all not care to hear or know
The sorrow of the ones below
We raise our trumpets up on high
In distant fields our battle's cry

We fight with minds of sharpened steel
Truth shall not intercept the deal

Lady walks in kismet's cloak
While we be very simple folk
There not be a night or day
That finds us asking for a fray
We work and toil and grind our teeth
We live too blind to give relief

Lady walks in madness
Lady takes to flight
Lady shrieks with gladness
Lady is a might not right

Not a lady for a kingdom
Not a lady for a crown
Just a little tattered remnant
Of the holy shroud

What joy will gossip strive to sting
What power is to clip her wing
Her temperament might be of child
Her come and go a bit too wild
Her dreams fantastic to your ill
Her ranting raven and full shrill

And all the town folk gather round
With stone and stick they strike her down
With shaven head and without dress
Commanded backward to the bench
The persecution of the court
And all because they see a wart
She looks too young she's still alive
Her lips they curl amidst the bile

Lady walks in madness
Lady takes to flight
Lady shrieks with gladness
Lady is a might not right
Not a lady for a kingdom, not a lady for a crown
Just a little tattered remnant of the holy shroud

Imaginary Conversations

Imaginary conversations
I have them often with you
A man of different persuasions
It's what intrigues me about you

You see the colour in the landscape
When all the rest see black and white
And just like me you have visions
In the empty sky at night

I see you too are a stranger
In this land we call our home
I see your feel they are restless
And long to leave this world alone

Enchanted Rivalry

You can leave me here alone
Forever waiting for your call
The love will keep the memory
Lit in the great dark hall

Our love I know is real
I saw it in it's flight
It flickered like a candle
On a balmy summer night

Dancing in your mirrors
That speak without your lips
My love your eyes say everything
The magic is at your fingertips

It is in the face of the boy
With a man locked deep within his soul
I try to pull him out, but the little boy won't let go

I am the spirit of the woman
Who longs to stop the wind
From blowing out the candles
That can warm their hearts again

Can you see her call for mercy
Fallen to her knee
Can you see her begging
For the opportunity
To set their hearts to dancing
In enchanted rivalry

The Oracle

I feel god's love
Streaming through my veins
Don't despair the broken path
Is leading with firm reins

Each step we take
So heavy in pain
Is to be relinquished
So the song may start again

A pinnacle, an oracle
An angel and a ghost
A lightening rod of energy
The delightful holy host

We are all channels for divinity
We open to receive
The voice of eternity

Cook the magic
Eat the spell
Delight in orgasm
Knowing well

Entice us god to be at peace
Know in all good time
Each soul will be released

Know that pain inside
You can't escape
It's part of being part of the human race
Perfection is a construct
A literal disease
When your heart is aching
Your on the high wire trapeze

Jesus, Allah, Buddha and Yahweh
Deities are multiple
Just as me and you

It's You

Of all my pictures
I don't have one with you
Of all my memories
I don't have one of you

I've searched every beach
Every face
Looked so hard
For a trace

Now I know
What I was looking for
Now I know
What I expected
To wash on my shore
It's you
What am I to do

I have to know

Sit beside
Tell me stories in your soft voice
Touch my hair
Let me know that you're there
It's your choice

Is this my life
Or is it all just a dream
This mystery
Is unravelling me

I'm looking for a clue
For a sign from above or below
I'm waiting on the will of heaven
Tell me how do I get there
I have to know

Do you know how to go to the place
Between the earth and the sky
Have you been to the land of mist
Where lost lovers cry

If you see my love along your way
Tell him I'm trying to get there
I'll find him someday

My five senses are stretched
To perceive what they can't see
I lie on my bed, try to pull him from ether into me

How do I make love with a being of light
How do I hold a lost dream in my arms at night

A Season for Waiting

You have to wait till the summer
When the warmth will calm the sea
You have to wait for the season
When the two can be set free

You know the truth inside you
It's fear and lies that lie before
There are many tests
Until you see the truth upon your door

No point in pushing quicker
The harder you pull, the farther it goes
The answer lies within the one unbroken strand
That binds the two untangled souls

From Atlantis to the deep south
There's been a chill wind blowing down this house
Your lost in the journey
Still you found your way
I came to earth to visit
To make the visit plain
I planted seeds of violence, to call your name
It is easier to get your notice
Because you live in a world of pain

There are many here among you
Who will try to stop the force
When you let it come through
It will be the best of course

Let it flow free, stop the panic
It is easier than you believe
Other people's pain, is not a part of you or me

You have to wait for the summer
When the warmth will calm the sea
You have to wait for the season
When the two shall be set free

Love is Everything

All in all
All is one
Love is everything as it's begun

Sweet tears of joy
Harsh voices rise
Was that fear I saw in your hesitant eyes

I miss you
You miss me
Were too proud, too proud to be

It's not natural to live this way
Longing and loving the years away

If I tell you my secrets
Will you keep them safe
If I take you with me, will you stop living like a waif
Like an angel without wings
A soldier without war
Like a lover without arms
A boat without oars
Like a preacher without book
A cook without the spoon
Like a butcher without boar
A song without a tune

Tantalus

As I stand at my kitchen window
As I lay myself to sleep at night
As I awaken still untethered
From the thoughts, that are racing round my head

I've become a hunter of reminders of you
Reading between your lines and reviews

Like Tantalus dying of thirst
Chest deep in water
I'm a hungry ghost
Haunting what is left of your world and mine

I used to be Her

She had a shrine of paintings on the wall
He sang to her at night
The guitar played by itself
As the lights flashed off and on

She cried for years
Listening to his songs
From dusk to dawn

I used to be her
That crazy girl
I used to be her

She tried to resurrect the dead
Most think it was all in her head
She had not found her knight and true
And in his ghostly image
She would invent
A lover who could not leave or be spent

Well if she isn't crazy
She is intoxicatingly so
If she isn't pretty
She's a pretty little mess
I'm told

The candles burned to fly
While everyone got high
Psychics came and went and warned
Be careful what you wish for
You might just get a reflection

She took a drunk in off the street
Cleaned him up as best she could to be neat
She lost it all
For the fantasy of resurrecting the dead
One lover lost on alcohol, the other lost in the sky
The youngest of the weedy lot, lost on pot

Well if she isn't crazy
She weaves a web
For dreamers in her bed

They say the price before 2000
Got too high, and on the beach
She built a funeral pyre
Tore the paintings off the wall
And burned them all
One full moon eclipse
In July

All That is Blue

Set aside all that is blue
Search your soul
For those who are true

Bless each day
When the sun shines through
Be grateful sweet Hazy
An angel has spoken to you

Put away your fears
Dry all of your tears
Lay your weary head upon my invisible breast

Know in your imperfect way
You are truly blessed

Becoming an angel
Is as easy as you let it be
To love an earthling
An impossible task
After knowing me

Dance, dance
In the dark and in the light
Hold your vices far and tight
Cradle your fears
And release them to the sky
Only one life is passing us by

I hold you when you're sleeping
I kiss you while you weep
I protect you while you drive,
so wild

Come sweet angel one of delight
The darkness is within the light

Maybe

I long to hear the music
Your voice above the waves
Your gentle eyes in lilac time
Your laughter in warm rain

I long to walk beside you
To hold your hand in mine
I feel your breath upon my cheek
Soft lips caressing thine

I can hold you in my heart
I feel you in the candle flame
But I can't see you with my eyes

Maybe you're my baby now
Maybe you're my neighbour's child
Maybe you are lost in the sky
Too far away to see
Maybe I'll learn how to fly
Maybe you'll visit in my dreams
Or maybe I'll just have to wait
Until the day I die

Printed in the United States
By Bookmasters